The Glass Jar

The Glass Jar

ROBERT MORRISON RANDOLPH

RESOURCE *Publications* · Eugene, Oregon

THE GLASS JAR

Copyright © 2024 Robert Morrison Randolph. All rights reserved. Except for brief quotations in critical publications or reviews, no part of this book may be reproduced in any manner without prior written permission from the publisher. Write: Permissions, Wipf and Stock Publishers, 199 W. 8th Ave., Suite 3, Eugene, OR 97401.

Resource Publications
An Imprint of Wipf and Stock Publishers
199 W. 8th Ave., Suite 3
Eugene, OR 97401

www.wipfandstock.com

PAPERBACK ISBN: 979-8-3852-1569-0
HARDCOVER ISBN: 979-8-3852-1570-6
EBOOK ISBN: 979-8-3852-1571-3

04/11/24

Contents

- I | 1
- II | 17
- III | 22
  - (Jar Poem 1) | 22
  - (Jar Poem 2) | 23
  - (Jar Poem 3) | 24
  - (Jar Poem 4) | 25
  - (Jar Poem 5) | 27
  - (Jar Poem 6) | 29
  - (Jar Poem 7) | 31
- IV | 33
  - (Shadow Poem 1) | 35
  - (Shadow Poem 2) | 36
  - (Shadow Poem 3) | 37
  - (Shadow Poem 4) | 38
  - (Shadow Poem 5) | 39
- V | 40
  - (Jar Poem 8) | 41
  - (Jar Poem 9) | 43
- VI | 46
  - (Jar Poem 10) | 47
  - (Jar Poem 11) | 48
  - (Jar Poem 12) | 49
  - (Jar Poem 13) | 51
  - (Jar Poem 14) | 55

I

Loving Lord, early April dogwoods
bloom among leafless oaks
and I walk at daybreak a shoreline path
by a deep pool of clear water.
I see bottom stones and brook trout.
This world is a fountain of sincerity
and your love is the soul of it all.

Thank you for the wavy grain pattern
in the walnut handle of my walking cane,
for the misty mountains beyond the river,
for the near and far, the puff of breeze
now rippling the water at first light.

Thank you for this day you have made,
for its coastlines around the Americas
and around each acorn under that oak tree.
Thank you for the presence of the stars
nightly bowing to the moon, and kneeling
to you. Thank you for the silver silence
of the gibbous moon whose arc of light
filled my bones last night. Thank you,
for your grace always bending toward me.

Father, you break my heart; thank you.
I give you my life, my body now frail
but my passion for you unabated.
Thank you for agedness, for those clouds
wispily dissolving above tilled fields.
Thank you for dirt and seeds, for all plants
in this thoughtful world where each leaf
reaches toward light. Every new day
I reach again for your light and grow
toward you. Thank you for every day.

Here the brook bends east, goes shallow
and flows over small stones. I stand still,
close my eyes and listen to the riffle.
My Lord, what a gift is this world!
The air here smells clean, gently polished,
smooth. Thank you for such clean air
and small stones in water flowing to the sea.

I owe you everything, including this breath,
this moment by this brook inside this day,
this life. You are thisness, hereness,
being, the great I Am, and all I am gives
you thanks. I am called to love you, my Lord,
to relationship, creative reaching for you.
To deny my calling to love you creatively
would build stasis in me equal to death,
as if the stream lost its source and dried up.

The brook flows into and out of itself
at any point of its being. I want to flow
in your love, thankful and serving others,
finding myself in prayer. I see the riffle
as symbolizing prayer, spoken *sotto voce*.

The path leads up the bank along a ledge
above the brook, then down again through
a patch of wood anemones, their faces always
turned to the sun. Such shy-seeming beauty
in this bare wood seems a tender mercy.
My Lord, thank you for exquisite gentleness,
the touch of love of your fingertips to guide,
to heal, to gently lift a grief-weighted soul.
May I keep turned to your love any flowers
my life may grow, or else they would die.

The beech tree ahead holds carvings,
names, initials inside hearts cut into the trunk.
I stop in its shade and find my initials
carved many years ago and now owned
by the tree's growth, dark scars
among many others. The breeze rustles
leaves and I feel prayerful. My Lord Jesus,
you bear the wounds of all our sins
and in return your love shelters us in peace
undeserved and beyond understanding.
Thank you for asking God, the Father,
to forgive us for wounding you. Thank you
for saying we did not know what we did.
I touch my carved initials in this tree
and know by loving you, believing in you,
Lord Jesus, I am forgiven for my sins.

I come to a simple stone bench I built
where I sit and try to come openly to you,
my Lord. This world is a house of arriving,
full of doorways nothing can destroy,
but I stay closed inside the narrow hallway
of myself, my humanity. I want to step
outside my bones and talk with you,
and then return to talk about you to others,
to help them truly live by loving you.

I watch water at the head of the pool
become two channels to go around a rock
and flow into one channel again below,
but there is against the downstream face
of the rock a small space of quiet water,
an abiding, seemingly meditative moment
in the flow, like a prayer inside a prayer,
a calm eye looking honestly into itself.
One year, spring floods left a kneeler,
a short log, tentatively settled behind the rock.

My Lord, Jesus, you are the rock
of my salvation and this rock in the brook
that day became my kneeling rock.
I took off my shoes and socks, rolled up my pants,
and waded out to the still eye of water.
I knelt facing upstream and put my palms
on the top of the rock and my forehead
on the backs of my hands. The water
flowed around me and I waited for you.

I thought of Mary of Magdala in the gospel
of John walking before dawn alone
to the tomb. If the Bible were a symphony
sometimes the full orchestra would voice
the moment, but Mary's pre-dawn walk
to the tomb would be one instrument,
maybe a guitar, or cello. When she found
the tomb empty, she wept, because
she did not know where they had taken him.
In that emptiness Jesus spoke to her.
I was one person kneeling in prayer
in a brook. I wanted to hear His voice,
or to feel lifted by your hand, my Lord.

I heard the water say its ongoing name.
I heard a blue jay carve its name in the air;
I heard wind rustle the ironwood leaves.
Was that your voice; was I in the palm of your hand
already? I felt your presence against my skin
like a touch, not a voice, a relationship too close
for words. I had felt it before while reaching for you,
unforgettable times, but there was always
a distance between us. You were so close,
and yet a boundary remained somehow.

I opened my eyes. I wanted to light a candle,
a soft flame, or wait for a temple bell
to toll, or easy rain to fall and bend me away
in its widening dream to the sea.
It was time to forgive everything. I felt
an arc of assurance, a touch. I could have
been grain in a burl wood table, or a whorl
of light. This was not the doorsill of dream,
rather a depth of wound. A beautiful silence
deeper than a mirror encircled my body.
The brook glowed with grace. The moment
was so real I thought my soul must have its own bones.

The brook flowed toward me.
It knew itself, its sorrow. A crow called
from the eastern bank, the deeper side.
I could have replied from some shadow
in my blood but I only wanted to listen
to the crow's call again, which seemed
a beautiful black flower. I gave thanks
for the brook. It gathered silences,
bits of moonlight, winter afternoons.
It had no choice but to believe in itself.
I felt full of clear light, gracious Lord,
as if you had whispered into my ear
my secret name pure just for that moment,
as passing and true as a shape of mist.

II

I sit in a rocking chair by a window
in my study, around me hundreds
of books filled with my marginalia,
my scholarly reaching for you, my Lord.
I think of Dante at the end of the *Paradiso*,
finally seeing your light and knowing
it surpassed all possible description,
yet knowing absolutely your full presence
had transformed his consciousness.
He described that certainty as waking
from a dream. I touch the window
with my fingertips and remember
a transformative dream of presence.

In my dream I sat in a straight-backed
Shaker chair by a window at night,
praying, and suddenly I became terrified
because I felt brightness as a presence
against my skin. I knew beyond reason
that a star was coming closer, rapidly.
I got up and knelt by the open window,
feeling panic and awe. I bowed my head
against the light's unbearable brightness
and I knew the starlike essence had come
to my window. It felt to me that the world
had gone still. From inside the light,
that perfect stillness of complete silence,
I heard an impossibly gentle voice say,
"Do not be afraid, I have something
for you to do." They felt like the only words
I had ever heard. There was no argument,
only experience. I fell into the silence
echoing around them it seemed like forever.
But then I felt the light begin again
to distance itself and I opened my eyes
to see the star all the way back in place
in the sky. I saw how it differed
from other stars by being not just light,
but living light. Then I awoke
feeling called to serve you, my Lord,
whether or not you sent the dream.

It might have been my reaching for you
that built that dream from within
my own bones, but my most ardent
argument for your presence in all things
could not create that voice. It was not
made of me, but of an intensity so still
in singularity I could not have directly
looked at it in the flesh of this world.
The words themselves felt like a wound
made of stillness, deep love, and light.
I understood that after his trip to Damascus
there was no use arguing with Paul
about the divinity of Jesus; there are words
that rechannel the blood into the heart.

Now, for me no two hours feel the same.
There is presence in all things, openness to you,
my Lord. I had a smaller dream, of an owl
in an oak watching me as I sat by the brook.
I knew the owl's bones were made of darkness,
but the owl's eyes were candles.
I thought that if I closed my eyelids to pray
my bones would light up. I know presence calls
to presence, deep to deep, and the holiness of life
is beyond naming, so at night I sit on the porch swing
listening to the voice of your light, not the stars,
but the light in my blood. We all have it,
your voice in our blood, to hold sacred.
May I learn to listen with all my life to your voice,
to have ears to hear, and courage and will
to sacrifice all that turns my heart from you.

I feel your presence like the voice in my dream,
powerfully here and yet beyond me.
My Lord Jesus, in you all things cohere
with complicacy beyond my finite grasp.
I reach into paradox, metaphor, image,
to move deeper into your presence and your love.
I stay awake in my cabin writing small poems
I put in glass jars. These are love poems
about moments of imagination in my world,
to you, from me. I shape them sculpturally,
trying to make them word sculptures of sharing.
These 14 poems, shapes of my loneliness,
reach out to your loving unbounded presence
from inside the song-spaces of my finitude.

III

(Jar Poem 1)

Tonight I feel
    lonely
like a white rose
      on a marble step.

I feel broken by loving you, my Lord.
If I could play guitar
how I feel, rain
      would fall around the moon.

(Jar Poem 2)

From my porch
I look at hilltops
    and I float over trees

  in the gondola
    of my body.

Across a cloudy sky
  a pair of geese flying
seem like ink

on papyrus,
    a psalm.

(Jar Poem 3)

Under the yard light
mist reaches out of itself
    like a sleeper
   trying to wake.

  I feel sad
because nothing knows how to look at itself,
    to find Jesus within.

  In that great wound
the wind suddenly stops, and I ask
if I have forgiven others
   enough.

    I turn from the window
   and see my body
in a cheval glass,
quiet bent all around my skin.
    I know I am in an eddy of God's love.

(Jar Poem 4)

I walk to the café
with a mirror of silence
*   inside me. I remember*

last night's moonlight
shining in the window. It could
*   have been a wild swan*
flying into its own heart.

*   To a brightening sky*
I pray, the words
circling around each other
*   like migrating cranes.*

I know my glass jar poems must fail,
falling back, as they must because of my finitude
only into themselves, but thank you
for letting me try to be with you, my Lord,
while knowing I cannot grasp beyond
the jars of my reaching.

(Jar Poem 5)

Tonight again
a dim mist-nimbus
　　　around the yard light
　a poem.

In these poems the word choices are mine,
the spaces are mine, and all are moments of my waiting
to know you better. They may not resemble
anyone else's moments of openness, and, of course,
they fail to bring the fire and the rose to oneness,
but they offer themselves in genuine reaching,
and, for me, closeness to you. You are the Creator.
We, in your image, also create in our reaching.
Forgive me if I try to break through boundaries.

(Jar Poem 6)

What happens
when I open my heart to the event
of these clouds?
There is nothing
that can take their place.

May some of the silences in my poetry
open space into my soul, a place of meeting you,
and let our meeting continue my creative longing.
Thank you for making me so that I live deepest,
most beautifully, artfully, and humanly in the suffering
of my reaching. The peace that surpasses all understanding
abides in my creative reaching to know you, while knowing
that in my finitude I must fail, and in my failure you love me.
Surely paradise for me cannot be static, but creative,
with eternal life being the reaching itself. Thank you
for making the boundary between us change
as I change, calling me to endless creative response
toward intimacy. Thank you for letting me find
and know my true self in loving you, reaching for you.

(Jar Poem 7)

Lonely rain
knelt
    before first light
        in prayer for all our wounds,

or so it seemed
to me. Thank you
    for the rain.

Intensity is all, in human art and loving you.
We all have something to do, love you wholly.
We shape our reaching, its passion, our longing,
into the deepest, pure, artful spaces we can
in order to wait for you. Some music makes me weep
in its beautiful humanity, as if in those very voices,
very instruments, very notes, selfhood is achieved
that opens deeply into your presence. Prayer,
or rather the silence inside prayer, also opens a door
into your presence, a deeper sense of connection.
Often, the spaces between words, lines, beats in poems
I write ask me to wait to know you better before
I continue. Thank you for giving us doorways of art.

IV

At one point, before the glass jar poems,
all I had was a quiet room on a farm,
forgetful rain, a stone barn echoing with broken hope,
and hand-cut cedar fence posts looking lonely.
I often walked to an abandoned house
and on past as a kind of salute, measuring
my life against broken windows, the rusted
well-pump handle, the unpruned peach trees.
I took photos of the barn door, the rusty hinges
and old wood. They seemed deposits of memory.
I started to walk into myself, and the deeper
I got, the more I looked around at the world.
Something seemed to be waiting for me.

I sometimes write poems left margin justified,
thick as shadows, shapes of my reaching
as always, hoping to create a place for us to meet,
yet inescapably enshadowed by my finitude.
Are they only for me? Are the shadow poems
at best sad, poorly formed pearls inside
my finite shell? I pray not so, because I write them
as reachings, my Lord, to make my limits
more porous. These shadow-form poems,
with few open spaces, reach to you in the dark.

(Shadow Poem 1)

In the orchard, the ice coated apple trees
appear deliquescent. Under the yard light
the stone wall falls into its own heart.
In winter everything falls slowly into itself.
Looking out the window I fall slowly into myself.
If I had an old silk robe I would wear it tonight.
On my robe I would want an embroidered dove
facing down, wings spread, above my heart.

(Shadow Poem 2)

Sometimes there can be a wind so dry
it is full of crucifixion streets. I can feel it
circling me. On the other hand, resurrection roads
do not end until they turn gold. I want to wear
a black cape and walk those gold roads toward sunset,
every shadow a forgiveness. On those days
I could be a beautiful broken fountain last light
keeps falling through, never forgetting me.

(Shadow Poem 3)

The manes of those black mares
gather last light at sunset. It must be so,
because I want to fly to them and stand with them
on that hilltop. We cannot choose whom to love.
With them there can be no echoes.
There are as pure as spaces between stars.
The field goes still as glass around them.
One lifts her head from the grass very slowly
as if into great nearness with the day's afterglow.
They could be letters written from God.
What do they do with their beauty until dawn?

(Shadow Poem 4)

A heron flies from the hill pond,
slow winged, neck arced down, over the fence line.
The bird seems a dream unfolding. Maybe I should
carry a lantern and walk at night facing Jerusalem.
Maybe I should buy a child a pinto pony.
The bird looks like a pure river of hope.
It flies past a small cove of light in the oak leaves.
If there can be a rainbow in a violin string, it is this heron
flying alone. Maybe honey can drip from a dream.
I think of Mary holding her child on her lap.

(Shadow Poem 5)

Old boards have leaned against the barn
for years, almost creatures longing for forgiveness.
I love them there, like artwork. They could be
a broken window in an abandoned cabin
where birds nest. They could be old men, magi,
walking long distances to see a baby.
One painted blue goes off by itself, like a blue star.
One is white like a feather fallen from the moon.
They could be angels, or stories that never got told.
They are old streets in a sincere town.
They want forgiveness for being so strong in themselves.
I want to leave them alone. They are old boards
trying to dream. Everything reaches toward you, my Lord.

V

Since my transformative dreams I have earned
academic degrees through a Doctor of Philosophy
in literature, and Masters of Arts in theology
and counseling. I have taught for 50 years
at the university level, pastored a congregation
and counseled homeless addicts. The dream voice
still lives in me, both stilling and calling me
deep in my bones. So I search for you, my Lord,
the searching a paradox, because you are always
here, every heartbeat, with me, with all of us.

(Jar Poem 8)

My Lord,
  I live inside my death
  carrying your eternal light
in the center of my hands.

  My bones are the sad
edges of my love
    for you.

Often, after my classes are over and the students
have left the room, I sit and recall the reaching
that took place. Reaching keeps us alive, our hearts open.
My Lord, do you reach also? I think you do, toward
us for our music, poetry, prayers, all sincere artworks
created to be with you, trying to requite your love.

(Jar Poem 9)

Many years ago
an oval shape
of afternoon sunlight fell
    on a narrow plank
hardwood floor

as my professor read a Hamlet
soliloquy

    and I looked at the floor
as at a soft, quiet star.
      You were so near.

    My life has been
like that, loving you
    from the start.

    Now I want to unlock
the barrier-door
    of disbelief in my students

 to reveal
the holy room
    in their bones
      where you wait.

Before one school day, there was a storm.
Broken off branches in my yard looked sad,
with only distant friends, if any. They had entered
a doorway of silence. It was too late at that point
for them to die thoughtfully or carefully, wet
and depressed as they were; and yet,
they were priceless with this world's destiny.
I improvised a blues tune on guitar
for the branches and for all my wrong turns
on back roads. My Lord, thank you
for all my wrong turns and sufferings
in reaching, guiding me deeper into myself and to you.
Thank you for your presence in all things.

In my teaching, after the storm I lectured
as I stood near a window. Every word
waited to be said carefully. I felt the surety
of my students' fragility, and mine,
and our need to die to our sins. I had another body
outside the window trying to get in.

VI

My Lord, I am an old man alive at the coastline
of my bones, trying to be with you by building
sanctuaries within poems. I do not know
if I have done the task you gave me, but your call
sharpened my eyesight and shaped my dreams.
Sometimes I feel smoothed, almost as polished
as a dove's call, because of your grace, my Lord,
your blessings. Sometimes I feel broken,
because of my choices, sometimes made of ashes.
Sometimes I cannot tell myself apart from myself.
Thank you for letting me reach for wholeness
through all of it, inside your abiding love.

(Jar Poem 10)

About past years
I remember images, shards of memory.
      Who was I then?

    Who am I, wholly, now?
I touch the mirror.
The lace curtains look thoughtful
      but unwilling to decide anything.

The incalculable loneliness of windows,
    a life of only transparency,
  no memory, no choices
or need for your love, no reaching.

    Those days I walked a country road
by a broken-windowed abandoned house.
      On cold days I saw my breath.
On clear nights
 I saw the stars.
I prayed.
      I saw the one star.

(Jar Poem 11)

Today I saw a blue heron
stand quiet as a glove
*　　　　and I felt distances inside the rain.*

The noun "rain"
contains a reaching,

always lost, trying to go home.

All nouns have verb-hearts,
*　　　　especially your divinity,*
*　　　　　　　my Lord.*

(Jar Poem 12)

Sometimes at night
 when I think of years ago
  it feels like a silver road inside the dark

leading to that shape of hope
again, on the farm.
  I remember
   doing dishes and looking at the roses
blooming outside.

In memory, I keep trying to get to
you, my Lord,
but I always
  come to those roses and the rain,
like a dead end,
a stone in the heart.

I also remember a field of wildflowers,
  as if growing at the boundary
of this world

with a presence
like a beautiful dream.
I prayed in that field
  many days at sunset

when I could feel so many things

drift out of themselves
openly,
a giving.

(Jar Poem 13)

These days
I look at my lily garden,
      drink green tea,
read poetry,
listen to Perlman play Brahms.

    A dark light
 bone deep, a presence
   beneath the spectrum
      of reason,
a living memory, a relationship,

      stays with me like a star
   both folded into itself,
and unfolding,

and there is at least an angel
inside the rain,
      who can turn all wounds
into doves,

who asks the night, like a friend,
      if the gloves of moonlight
can touch me
as lovingly
     as they touch the sea.

Years ago I stood on the Maryland shore
looking west across Chesapeake Bay,
and a bald eagle flew so low overhead
I heard the down strokes of the wingbeats
and felt the silences as the wings reached up.
All I ever truly have to give is the now,
this moment, without comment beyond itself,
only in itself, of itself, the now of my reaching,
of faith, which can abide in the current word
in a poem, in a student's, counselee's,
or congregant's voice, or the space before that word,
all the flowing moments of being inside
your holy presence, my Lord, as when today
this room suddenly filled with tender light
in the silence behind the rain and I reached for you,
lifting all my life to thank you for all my life.

And now, near the end of this poem,
I sit quietly in last light when things fit together
gently. Dim shadows seem shy, sincere.
The brook holds secret light. The moon rises.
In the dark, with no lamps or candles, the room
soft with night, I leave the back door open
to hear the crickets. I center myself and pray.

Deep silence, a corolla of peace, gathers
around my bones as always when I pray
because I love you, my Lord. In this tender,
broken life behind my closed eyes I want to
be with you wholly, to reach in prayer
beyond tonight's waning gibbous moon
to walk with you by a river of perfect light.

(Jar Poem 14)

Ducks fly across a gray sky
on a cold day,

The birds
drag anchors through my heart
*   and another life gathers around me,*
*   another life,*
a boundary of nearness.

www.ingramcontent.com/pod-product-compliance
Lightning Source LLC
Chambersburg PA
CBHW061252040426
42444CB00010B/2360